Andrew Dickson White

European Schools of History and Politics

Andrew Dickson White

European Schools of History and Politics

ISBN/EAN: 9783337086251

Printed in Europe, USA, Canada, Australia, Japan

Cover: Foto ©Paul-Georg Meister /pixelio.de

More available books at **www.hansebooks.com**

JOHNS HOPKINS UNIVERSITY STUDIES
IN
HISTORICAL AND POLITICAL SCIENCE

HERBERT B. ADAMS, Editor

History is past Politics and Politics present History—*Freeman*

FIFTH SERIES

XII

EUROPEAN SCHOOLS

OF

HISTORY AND POLITICS

BY ANDREW D. WHITE

BALTIMORE
N. MURRAY, PUBLICATION AGENT, JOHNS HOPKINS UNIVERSITY
DECEMBER, 1887

COPYRIGHT, 1887, BY N. MURRAY.

JOHN MURPHY & CO., PRINTERS,
BALTIMORE.

TABLE OF CONTENTS.

	PAGE.
EUROPEAN SCHOOLS OF HISTORY AND POLITICS:	
In Germany	7–11
In Austria-Hungary	11–12
In Switzerland	12
In France	12–17
In Italy	17–21
APPLICATION OF EUROPEAN EXPERIENCE TO OURSELVES	21–44
MODERN HISTORY AT OXFORD, BY W. J. ASHLEY	45–55
RECENT IMPRESSIONS OF THE ÉCOLE LIBRE, BY T. K. WORTHINGTON	56–67
PREPARATION FOR THE CIVIL SERVICE IN GERMAN STATES, BY L. KATZENSTEIN	68–75
LIST OF BOOKS UPON THE GERMAN CIVIL SERVICE, BY L. KATZENSTEIN	75–76

EUROPEAN SCHOOLS

OF

HISTORY AND POLITICS.[1]

In various visits to European universities during the past thirty-five years, I have been especially interested in this department, embracing those studies by which men are fitted to take part in public affairs, and I purpose giving a general account of its recent growth and present condition at some of the centers of European instruction, and then to bring the knowledge thus obtained to bear on what seems a great practical need in our own country.

GERMANY.

In every important university in Europe, during many years past, extended courses of instruction in history, political and social science, and general jurisprudence have been presented. The foremost rank hitherto, in this instruction, has

---

[1] A portion of this paper was read at the third anniversary of the Johns Hopkins University, February 22, 1879, and was then printed as read. The whole study is so important to students and teachers of History and Politics in this country that the Editor of this Series requested President White to allow a partial revision of the subject matter and its reproduction in the present form, with certain timely supplements which show what work is actually in progress to-day in European Schools of History and Politics.—*Editor.*

been taken by Germany. While it is true that the want of practical political instruction, that which comes by taking part directly in political affairs, has stood in the way of a complete, well-rounded political education of the whole people in that country, it is also true that to these courses is due almost entirely that excellence in German administration which is at last acknowledged by the entire world. We may disbelieve in the theories of government prevalent among the Germans, but we cannot deny their skill in administration.

Among the German institutions, in which a leading place is given to instruction relating to public affairs, probably the most interesting is the University of Tübingen.

Several years ago far-seeing statesmen established there a distinct faculty, devoted to the training of men for the service of the state. The results are now before the world. The graduates of this department hold to-day leading places not only in the administration of the Kingdom of Würtemberg, but throughout the German Empire. In conversation with leading men in Southern Germany, I have not found one who has not declared this and similar courses of instruction a main cause of the present efficiency in the German administration.

The faculty at Tübingen, dealing practically and directly with political and social instruction [*Staatswirthschaftliche Facultät*], in the years 1887–88 embraced nine professors, besides sundry associate instructors, and in the faculties of law and philosophy were several other professors constantly giving instruction bearing upon these subjects. From their courses of lectures, recently announced, I select the following:

1. Political economy.
2. Money.
3. Postal and railroad system.
4. Labor question.
5. Agricultural policy.
6. Forestry (5 and 6 connected with excursions).
7. Credit and banking.
8. Finance.

9. Corporations.
10. Social statistics.
11. General constitutional law and politics.
12. German constitutional law.
13. Administrative law and practice, including dealings with crime.
14. International law.
15. The philosophy of law.
16. History of communism and socialism.
17. Educational system of modern States.
18. Greek and Roman institutions.
19. History of the age of Reformation.
20. Universal history.
21. Constitutional history of Germany (since 1806).
22. History of the German Empire since 1871.
23. History of our own times since 1850.
24. History of social revolutions of modern times.
25. Exercises in the seminary of political economy.
26. Exercises in the seminary of history.

Theses for competition (" Preisaufgaben ") :

1. The question of the dwellings of the laborers and the attempts at solving it.

2. Representation of the influence of Albrecht Thaer and Justus Liebig on the development of German agriculture.

The above selection is made to show the extent of the instruction. There are also many other lectures in other faculties on kindred topics. It should also be noted that these are the subjects presented in a single term of a single year. During the time given by the student to his university course many other important subjects would be taken up.

The University of Tübingen may be taken as a type of those institutions in Central Europe which group studies relating to public affairs [*Staats- und Cameralwissenschaft*] in a single faculty; but in most of the universities these studies are not thus grouped, but simply scattered through various faculties, and especially through those of law and philosophy.

Of this latter class of institutions the **University of Berlin** may be taken as typical. From the courses given through the year **1887–88** I select the following, to show the scope of instruction:

1. Political economy.
2. Finance.
3. Banking.
4. Money.
5. Administration.
6. Taxation with the Romans.
7. Agricultural policy.
8. Statistics.
9. **Socialism** and Individualism.
10. History of the Middle Ages **(4 different courses).**
11. Prussian history.
12. Politics.
13. Parliamentarism.
14. History of East and Middle Asia in the 19th century.
15. History of the Macedonian Empire.
16. Roman history since Nero's death.
17. Greek and **Roman** institutions.
18. Geography.
19. Constitutional history of Germany (2 different courses).
20. Modern history (3 different courses).
21. Sources of Greek history.
22. History of the Roman Empire.
23. History of the Popes.
24. Exercises in the seminaries, besides lectures on the various subjects of law.

Connected with this in the announcement were grouped a number of those studies which with us are generally brought into the courses of our agricultural colleges. In such universities as Leipzig, Bonn, Heidelberg, Gœttingen, Jena, Kœnigsberg, Marburg, &c., similar provisions were made. It is interesting to observe that in all these the professors were ready to grapple with living questions, and that courses were given in nearly all of them by distinguished men upon questions raised by the socialistic party.

As regards the preparation of young men for these courses, it is certainly not more than equivalent to that obtained in American colleges and universities of a good grade by the end of the freshman year. Having heard recitations of classes in various departments of the German gymnasia, or preparatory colleges, I make this statement with confidence.

Austria-Hungary.

In the Austrian Empire the new and liberal government has carried out largely the same system.

The announcement of the University of Vienna for 1887–88 shows that it has adopted the Tübingen plan of a distinct faculty for subjects relating to political and social science. In one term of 1887–88 courses of lectures were presented by this faculty, from which I select the following:

Vienna, 1887–88 (including two Semesters).

1. History of German Empire and law (3 different lectures).
2. Constitutional law of Austria.
3. Penal law and prisons.
4. Church law.
5. Roman law.
6. Law of inheritance.
7. The philosophy of law.
8. Law of mining.
9. Labor legislation.
10. Finance.
11. Political economy.
12. Statistics.
13. Administration.

Besides this, provision was made in other faculties for extensive instruction in various departments and periods of history.

As to the general character of all this instruction among German-speaking peoples, whatever it may have been in the past, it is not at present calculated to breed *doctrinaires*; it is large and free; the experience of the whole world is laid under contribution for the building up of its students; questions of living interest have their full share in the various lecture-rooms. To know how our own democracy is solving its problems, one of the German universities sends to this country for study one of its most gifted professors, one from whom thinking men on this side of the Atlantic have been glad to learn the constitutional history of their own country. The lectures of Professor Von Holst, as delivered here, and his work upon the constitutional history of the United States, are sufficient to show that this instruction in the German universities is given in a large way, and is not made a means of fettering thought. At no seats of learning in the world, probably, is political thought more free. The University of Berlin stands on the main avenue of the capital of the German monarchy, directly opposite the Imperial Palace. Within a stone's throw of the Emperor's work-table are the lecture desks of a large number of professors, who have never hesitated to express their views fully upon all the questions arising between democratic and monarchical systems; I have myself, in these lecture-rooms, heard sentiments freely uttered which accorded perfectly with the ideas of Republican and Democratic American statesmen.

SWITZERLAND.

In the Swiss Republic, instruction in political and social science is held in especial honor. At the universities of Zurich, Basle, Berne, and Geneva, a large number of professors are constantly engaged in it; young men come to them with the direct purpose of fitting themselves for a political career.

FRANCE.

In France, for many years, history, political and social science and general jurisprudence have held a leading place in all the great institutions for higher instruction. Whatever may have been the political mistakes of that country, many of which are directly traceable to the want of popular education, it cannot be denied that the internal administration of the country is conducted with great ability, and its ordinary legislation with great foresight. The financial errors which in times gone by have cost France so dear, and which have since been so ruinous to other nations, have been skilfully avoided during this century. It is common to ascribe the speedy recovery of France from various catastrophes to the subdivision of land among her people. This is doubtless an important factor in her success, but it is by no means all; a similar subdivision of land in our own country has produced no such rapid recovery from financial disease. No one can read French discussions of economic questions without seeing that to the trained skill of her statesmen is in very great measure due that stimulus to the production of wealth, and that recuperative power after disaster, which astonished the world after 1870–71, and which present the financial history of the French Republic in such striking contrast to our own.

To these results have contributed in no small degree the courses at the College of France. At that institution, in the heart of Paris, a knot of men has long been giving the highest political and historical instruction. In the center stood Laboulaye, who, though later somewhat withdrawn by his duties in the French senate, during many years, delivered lectures, not only upon general political history, and especially upon the constitutional history of the United States, but upon comparative legislation. About him have stood such men as Wolowski, Chevalier, Levasseur, Franck, Maury, Rozière, the younger Guizot, and others, treating of various great historical, political, and social questions, presenting the best thoughts of the past and present. Among the courses of lectures at the College of France, I noted especially the following:

1. International law.

2. Comparative history of legislation.
3. Political economy.
4. History of economic doctrines.
5. History and morals.
6. History of political literature.

At the Sorbonne and various institutions throughout France, as at Dijon, Caen, Poictiers, Bordeaux, Grenoble, Toulouse, Rennes, Aix, and others, similar instruction, in a greater or less degree, is presented by vigorous men.

But perhaps the most interesting creation of the last 25 years, as regards the preparation of young men for the service of the state, is the Independent School of Political Sciences. At the head of this stands M. Boutmy as director, and about him have stood several of the most thoughtful and energetic men in France. Of these may be mentioned such as Léon Say, member of the Institute of France, senator and ex-cabinet minister, Leroy-Beaulieu, Roederer, Levasseur, Lyon-Caen, Ribot, De Foville, chief of the bureau of statistics in the ministry of finance, and others noted as members of the Institute of France, and of various important political bodies.

Independent School of Political Sciences at Paris.

PROGRAMME OF LECTURES OF TWO YEARS: 1887–88, 1888–89.

1. Comparative administrative organization.
2. Administrative affairs.
3. Financial systems of the principal nations.
4. Public revenues and taxation.
5. Political economy.
6. Statistics, foreign commerce.
7. Constitutional law of France, England and United States.
8. Constitutions of Germany, Austria, Belgium, Switzerland and Italy.
9. Parliamentary and legislative history of France, 1789–1875.
10. Geography and Ethnography.

11. Diplomatic history from 1789 to our own time.
12. Contemporary Europe and Oriental affairs.
13. Diplomatic history from 1648 to 1789.
14. Economic geography.
15. International law.
16. Comparative commercial and maritime law.
17. French colonial legislation.
18. Comparative civil legislation.
19. Colonial geography.
20. History of the formation of the principal states of Europe in the middle ages.
21. History of relations between the Occidental States and the Oriental.
22. Money and Banking.
23. Organization of the Central government.
24. Finance.

The whole of this instruction is divided into five sections. They are known as—

1. Section of administration.
2. Section of diplomacy.
3. Section of political economy and finance.
4. Section of colonial policy.
5. General section, including public law and history.

In addition to these, and connected with both, is "a course in modern languages," the two on which especial stress is laid being German and English.

While the purpose of this school is to prepare young men, in a general way, for public affairs, it has immediately in view preparation for certain branches of the administration under the French civil-service system. Each of the sections completely prepares for one of the following departments and their competitive examinations:

1. Diplomacy (ministry of foreign affairs, legations, consulates).
2. Council of State (auditorship of second class).
3. Administration, central and departmental (under prefectures, secretaryships of departments, councils of prefectures).

4. Inspection of Finances.
5. Court of Claims.
6. Colonial service in its various departments.

Besides it prepares for certain high positions in commercial life (banks, secretaryships of companies, inspection of railways, etc.)

This system of instruction presupposes the average secondary education, which may be considered practically equivalent to that given up to the end of the first year in our better colleges. The regular course of instruction in these schools is arranged to extend through two years.

A very interesting indication of the results obtained in this school is seen in the official statement regarding the success of its graduates in taking positions in the French administration under the civil-service rules. From the public competitive examinations, the following appointments have resulted:

Council of State.

1877–1887.—Of 60 candidates appointed, 48 belonged to this school.

Inspection of Finances.

1877–1887.—Of 42 candidates appointed, 39 belonged to this school. Since 1880 all the candidates appointed have been prepared by this school.

Court of Claims.

1879–1886.—Of 17 candidates, 16 belonged to this school.

Ministry of Foreign Affairs.

1886 and 1887.—Of 26 candidates appointed, 20 belonged to this school.

It will be seen, then, that this school, founded with an independent organization by a number of energetic scholars and political men, is already beginning to place its graduates in leading positions under the French Government, and to act with force upon the amelioration of the French public service.

No one will wonder at these results who has conversed with the professors and students. If in the lecture-room of the College of France, at various visits during the last quarter of a century, I have admired the impulse given to general political thinking, I have admired not less in this newly founded school of political science the directness with which the best thought is applied to the immediate needs of the nation. Besides this, the French Government has taken pains that such instruction shall be brought to bear upon men in training for the great industries of the country. Wolowski, distinguished throughout Europe as a political economist, was employed to give lectures upon political economy at the Conservatory of Arts and Trades [*Conservatoire des Arts et Métiers*]. He was succeeded by Professor Levasseur, of the Institute, and rarely have I seen an audience so attentive as the body of workingmen which fills his lecture-room. Lectures were also given by M. Burat in industrial economy and statistics.

ITALY.

In the universities of Italy, studies in political and social science and general jurisprudence have long been prominent. By the triumphs of Beccaria, Filangieri, and their successors, a great impulse was given to these subjects, and to this, probably, more than to anything else, is due the skill of Italian political management during the trying times of the last twenty years.

For a quarter of a century there had not been any striking increase in the number of persons engaged in teaching these subjects, but there has been great progress, notwithstanding. In a third visit recently made to several Italian universities, and among others to those of Naples, Pisa, Padua, and Bologna, I found a new scholastic atmosphere. When, over thirty years ago, I entered some of them for the first time, I was

struck with the listlessness, the trifling, the dalliance with
what may be called the mere fringes of civilization, and, as a
consequence, with the waste of vigorous thought; but as I
stood again in some of those lecture-rooms, in the midst of a
crowd of young men intently listening to lectures upon history,
political economy, and kindred subjects, I could see that Rossi,
Settembrini, Villari, Mancini, Pierantoni, De Gubernatis, and
their compeers, had not labored in vain—that the country
was aroused to the necessity of training up a body of men
fitted to continue the work of Cavour, D'Azeglio, and Ratazzi.
Especially valuable is the work begun and maintained under
the direction and by the munificence of the Marquis Alfieri di
Sostegno at Florence. His patriotism and filial love were
combined in this school for instruction in political science
and its influence upon his country, for good, is already felt.
The higher instruction in Italy suffers undoubtedly from the
scattering of resources through a multitude of universities;
still the provision in the best of them is by no means small.
In the University of Rome, which may be taken as a type, we
found the following studies:

1. The philosophy of history.
2. General geography.
3. International law.
4. Roman law.
5. Philosophy of law.
6. Political economy.
7. Introduction to the study of jurisprudence.
8. Diplomacy and the history of treaties.
9. History of law.

Great Britain.

The tendency toward strengthening this side of the higher
education is also evident in the English universities; perhaps
in none is the change within the last quarter of a century more
striking. My first visit to them was made over thirty years

ago. The provision at that time for instruction in political and social science, to say nothing of the natural sciences, was wretchedly inadequate. Now, although they fall far short of what they should be, the influence of such men as Whewell, Arnold, Smythe, Sir James Stephen, Goldwin Smith, Charles Kingsley, Thorold Rogers, Montague Bernard, Harcourt, Jevons, Stubbs, Freeman, Seeley, Bryce, Fawcett, and their associates, has told for good upon the generation which is beginning to take hold of public affairs.

It is true that there is not yet at the English universities at any one time any such extended faculty in this department as we find in the great institutions of France and Germany, but these subjects are beginning to assert themselves, and already concessions have been made to them by the university authorities in the matter of examinations and degrees which a quarter of a century ago the most sanguine could not expect.

Nor is this all; the more recently founded public schools, or, as they might be called, preparatory colleges, are directing much attention to the fitting of men for the public service. Under the new civil-service system of the British Empire, such training has received a great impulse. In its whole development throughout the lower colleges and the universities it is becoming more and more prominent, and the same tendency is clearly seen in the leading universities of Scotland.

Having thus called attention to the main lines on which this department of instruction has been developed, I would briefly point out what seems to me a very suggestive characteristic of the instructing bodies.

Whenever a faculty of instruction is entirely made up of men held aloof from the usual currents of public life, there is danger of doctrinairism and pedantry, if not of cynicism. But this European instruction in political and social science seems to have steadily warded off these evils.

The cause of this will be easily found, I think, by any one who will study the lists of professors. In every great nation of Europe it will be seen that in these faculties there is a considerable number of professors who, while carrying on their university duties, take an active part in public affairs. Professor Faweett, of Cambridge, was a most energetic member of the British Parliament; Professor Montague Bernard, of Oxford, was hardly less energetic in the diplomatic service; Professor Vernon Harcourt, of Cambridge, has shown himself a statesman in the parliament and in the cabinet; Professor Goldwin Smith, formerly of Oxford, has exercised a constant influence as a debater and writer in centers of political activity. Professor Bryce is a member of Parliament and has held an important Under-Secretaryship.

In France, among professors now in service, in addition to others already mentioned, such men as Flourens, Dunoyer, Foville, Machart, Colmet, Vergniaud, and many others, have been actively engaged in various important departments of the public service.

In Germany, we may name out of a multitude who, as active men of affairs, have brought into the lecture room new currents of thought from the world outside, such men as Heffter, Gneist, Bluntschli, Knies, Roscher, Wagner, Holst, Oncken, and many others.

In Italy, the active interchange between professorial and public life is even more striking; every new ministerial cabinet shows a strong representation from the great instructing bodies, and we constantly see leading men speaking, during one part of the year, from their seats as senators and deputies, and during another part from their professorial chairs at the various universities.

By this rapid summary, from which I have attempted to exclude confusing details as much as possible, it will be seen that the leading nations of Europe, republics as well as monarchies, have committed themselves fully to the idea that the service of the state requires a large body of men carefully and thoroughly trained; that in consequence a system of higher instruction has been adopted to meet the needs of those nations in this respect, and that the higher instruction has been kept in the current of the national life.

Application of European experience to ourselves.

I now turn to the practical application of this European experience and the modification of European methods with reference to the development of a system of instruction directly bearing upon public life in our own country.

The demand of this nation for men trained in history, political and social science, and general jurisprudence, can hardly be overstated.

In the United States we have, first of all, the national Congress, composed of two bodies, each called upon to discuss and decide the most important political questions, and to some extent the most important social questions. They thus discuss and decide for a nation, to-day of sixty millions of people, and which many now living will see numbering a hundred millions. Nor is it alone the appalling element of numbers which strikes the thoughtful citizen. Time stretches before us in a way even more appalling; foundations are now laying for centuries; what is done now is to tell for good or evil upon a long line of generations.

Nor is this all; the nations of the earth may be divided into active and passive. Active nations are those which are to work out the development of the world by thought and by act, by the speech and the book, by the missionary and the soldier, by the machine and the process—nay, by mere bales and boxes; passive nations are those which are to be acted upon, and often in ways more or less brutal. For good or evil, ours is to be among the active nations; its influence is to be felt not only upon the hundred millions of its own citizens, but upon the still greater number of the human race outside its boundaries.

Besides the Congress of the United States, we have nearly forty State legislatures, each composed of two houses, and besides these, county boards, town boards, and municipal councils innumerable.

There are also executive officers corresponding to these legislative assemblies, and all these, whether entrusted with executive or legislative functions, are called upon to think out and work out these problems, probably for the greater part of the human race.

Besides these regularly constituted bodies, there are, from time to time, constitutional conventions in the various States, fixing the basis of legislation; these exercise an influence exceedingly far reaching, for they discuss political and social questions with especial reference to the past experience and future needs of the country; they fix the grooves, they lay the track in which political and social development will largely run.

Not less important are certain other bodies, having a more profound influence on real legislation than men usually suspect; despite the theoretical separation of powers in our government, the judicial body, throughout this land, is, in a certain sense, a legislative body; judge-made law is felt throughout our system and always will be felt; the judiciary of this country, from the honored bench sitting at the Capitol to the multitude of State courts of every grade, has an influence far outreaching the settlement of transient questions in accordance with recognized legal principles; for good or evil, their ideas of public policy are knit into the whole political and social fabric of the future. The relations of capital to labor, the connection of production with distribution, education, taxation, general, municipal, and international law, pauperism, crime, insanity, all are constantly coming before these bodies; policies are fixed, institutions created, laws made with reference to all these questions—policies, institutions, laws, in which lie the germs of glory or anarchy, of growth or revolution.

More important in some respects than the demand for better political training, among those destined for the public bodies, is the demand by the press. Even those of us who had best realized the immense grasp which the newspaper press has upon modern civilization, were amazed, during the Expositions at Philadelphia, Paris, and New Orleans, at the revelations of the extent to which newspaper publishing is now carried.

When it is considered that at each of these myriad presses a knot of men is teaching large bodies of citizens, especially as to their rights and duties in society, and advising them on the most important political and social questions, it will be seen that here is an enormous demand for men trained in the subjects already referred to.

That there is not sufficient training of this kind at present is lamented by none more than by the leading editors of our greater journals; it has passed into a proverb among them, that it is easier to obtain a score of men with striking ability as versifiers, novelists, critics, and humorists, than one man who can write brief, pithy, comprehensive articles on living questions.

The pulpit too, honored as it is throughout our land, and pledged to every form of humane work, is acknowledged by those who most adorn it to need greatly this same instruction. The charities of our cities are dispensed largely through church organizations, and those who have attended meetings of the Social Science Association of the United States will remember the lament of one of the most honored divines of the American pulpit at the mistakes made in these charities, and in other dealings with pressing social questions in which the clergy are greatly interested.

That there is a constant danger of error in the present is shown by the experience of the past.

There is no nation in the world to-day which is not suffering from the mistakes of law-makers on all these questions; no thoughtful student in social science is ignorant that education has been crippled by ill-studied institutions; that pauperism has been increased by the very legislation intended to alleviate it; that up to a recent period insanity was aggravated, and even made incurable, by the usual system of public provision; that ill-advised systems of warding off popular distress —systems embodying what is called "good common-sense"— have again and again brought great populations to the verge of starvation, and sometimes to the reality of it; and that down to a period within the memory of men now living, crime was rendered more virulent by the repressive system of every civilized country.

In the midst of this necessity for thought and care, how stands it with our own legislation? It was recently remarked by one of the most able and devoted men who ever left a foreign country to do noble work in this, that it saddened him to see many of the same lines of policy adopted in America that had brought misery upon Europe; to see the same errors in the foundation of these new states which have brought such waste and disaster and sorrow in those old states.

No one who knows anything of our legislation can deny that serious mistakes are constantly made, and often with the best intentions. Of course I do not pretend that there are not many excellent public servants who obtain their knowledge of political and social questions in later life; nor do I claim at all that none but men educated in these questions should enter public life; nor do I deny the great service of many men who have received no such training—recent events have revealed many such; but more and more, as civilization advances, social and political questions become complex; more and more the men who are to take part in public affairs need to be trained in the best political thinking of the world hitherto, need to know the most important experiences of the world, need to be thus prepared by observation and thought to decide between old solutions of state problems or to work out new solutions.

It will hardly be denied that the want of such knowledge and such training is seriously felt in all parts of the country. In various constituted bodies, theories have been proposed which were long ago extinguished in blood; plans solemnly considered which have led, without exception, wherever tried, to ruin, moral and financial; systems adopted which have been sometimes the tragedies, sometimes the farces upon the stage of human affairs.

All this, too, not mainly by knaves or fools, but often by men of vigorous minds, of considerable reading, of what is called good common sense.

As to State legislation, we note a prodigious amount of waste and error in dealing with political and social questions. Institutions for the poor, the insane, the inebriates, the criminals, are constantly created at vast expense, yet often so placed and built and organized as to thwart their highest purposes. Laws for the repression of crime are often discussed with an utterly inadequate knowledge of principles, that in some other lands have been carefully settled; in questions of taxation, the settled experience and simplest reasonings and conclusions of thoughtful men in various nations often pass for nothing, and a spirit of anarchy results, only equaled by that of France just before the revolution of 1789; as regards pauperism, means are often taken similar to those which in England, over 300 years ago, began the creation of a permanently pauperized class; in dealing with education, codes are made and millions voted with no thorough discussion, and the relations of education to industry, the problem now occupying every other great nation of the earth, argued with far less care than the location of a canal bridge.

In county, town, and municipal bodies the same thing is hardly less glaring; almost every municipal abuse which Arthur Young found in France under Louis XVI., and which May found in England under George III., seems to find its counterpart somewhere in our own land and time. In one of the most enlightened counties of one of our most enlightened States, a body of excellent reputation and sound common sense has, at large expense, for years and years, kept up an institution, not merely for the punishment of old criminals, but for the development of new criminals; it has resisted, and is steadily resisting to-day, any movement to prevent the institution being what it has long been—a criminal high school, taking large numbers of novices and graduating them masters of criminal arts. And such institutions are to be found probably in every State in the Union.

This is not on account of want of integrity or capacity in the body concerned; it is composed of men who manage their own affairs honestly and prudently; but there is probably not one among them who has ever seen any discussion of the best modes of dealing with crime in civilized nations.

But let us leave the various constituted bodies and go among the people at large. In a republic like ours, the people are called on at the last to decide upon all fundamental questions; on their decision rest the strength, the progress, nay, in many cases, the existence of the republic.

To any such proper discussion and adjustment of political and social questions by the people there are two conditions: first, there must be education of the mass of the citizens, at least up to a point where they can grasp simple political questions; that is, up to the ability to read, to concentrate and exercise their reasoning powers on simple problems, and to know something of their own country and its relations to the world about it.

Such an education is given in the public schools of our country; with such a basis, the first great element in the safety of the nation is reasonably secure. I am convinced that such an educated democracy is the best of all bodies to which general public questions can be submitted, and for this belief there is high authority where we might little expect it: the recent utterances of leading statesmen and thinkers in England regarding the submission of questions of fundamental policy to a fairly educated people, as compared with the submission of such questions simply to the most highly educated classes, are very striking; the most thoughtful contemporary English statesman has declared that the judgment of the mass of the English voters on the leading political and social questions of the past fifty years has been far more just than that of the most highly educated classes, and he brings to the support of this statement historical arguments which cannot be gainsaid.[1]

As to this first condition, the general education of the people, we have made in most of our States large provision. I do not contend that our primary education is perfect; its imperfections are evident, but the people are awake to its importance, and show on all sides a desire to continue it; of course, demagogues here and there, seek to gain bits of special favor by attempting to undermine the system, but their tendencies are well known, and are steadily becoming better known.

The second condition of the proper maintenance of the republic, is suitable instruction for the natural leaders rising from the mass. The rise of such leaders is inevitable; they are sure to appear in every sphere of political and social activity; they come from all classes, but mainly from the energetic, less-wealthy classes, from the classes disciplined to vigor and self-denial by poverty.

These are to influence the country in all executive, legislative and judicial positions; they are to act in the forum and through the press; nay, perhaps more strongly still, by stimulating that imitation which a recent writer has shown to be one of the most powerful factors in the development of nations to higher political and social life.[2]

For the development of these with reference to this leadership, for the training of their powers of observation and reasoning, for the giving of that historical knowledge of past failures which is the best guarantee for future success, there is at present in our higher education in the United States no adequate provision. The educational exhibits at the Expositions at Philadelphia, Paris, and New Orleans show that here and there, in a few of our higher institutions, beginnings have been made, and good beginnings; but such institutions are few; in most of them political economy is not taught save by

---

[1] See the articles of Mr. Gladstone in "The Nineteenth Century," 1877-78.
[2] See Walter Bagehot, "Physics and Politics."

a short course of recitations from a text-book; in very few of them is there the slightest instruction, worthy of the name, in history—the very department which, in the European universities, is made to give a basis and a method for studies in political and social science.

The results of this defect in our higher education are constantly before us; among these natural leaders in our country, whether in the public assemblies or the press, there is certainly no lack of talent, and even genius; among the most striking characteristics of the country, as noticed by unprejudiced foreigners, is the great number of men of ability in every direction, and the power with which they are able to present their ideas to their fellow-citizens. But how is this power exercised? With few exceptions, the presentation of political and social questions at public meetings is even less satisfactory than in our representative bodies; the speakers generally have ability, but rarely have they studied the main questions involved; what they know has been mainly gathered here and there at hap-hazard, from this magazine and that newspaper; the result is natural; instead of real argument, too often invective; instead of illustration, buffoonery; instead of any adequate examination of the history involved, personal defamation; instead of investigation of social questions, appeals to prejudice.

It may be said that the cause of this lies in the natural tendency of democracy from the days of Cleon before the Athenian Assembly, to the gyrations of sundry politicians before certain American assemblies. This theory is easy and convenient, but any one much accustomed to public meetings in our country can see many reasons for disbelieving it; an American assembly enjoys wit and humor keenly; but there is one thing that it enjoys more, and that is the vigorous, thorough discussion of pressing political or social questions. The history of the past few years gives striking examples of this; not long since several statesmen of very different views, but powerful and thoughtful, went before large public meetings lamenting the fact that the questions discussed were questions of finance—the very dryest in political science; and yet those large audiences were held firmly from first to last by their interest in vigorous argument.

I am convinced that the difficulty is not in the want of popular appreciation of close argument, but rather in the frequent want among political leaders of adequate training for discussion.

The question now arises what this training in political and social science should be.

I answer first, that there should be close study of the political and social history of those peoples which have had the most important experience, and especially of our own; thus alone can the experience of the past be brought to bear upon the needs of the present; thus alone can we know the real defeats and triumphs of the past, so that we may avoid such defeats and secure such triumphs in the future.

In the next place, I would urge the teaching of political economy in its largest sense, not the mere dogmas of this or that school, but rather the comparative study of the general principles of the science as laid down by leading thinkers of various schools; and to this end, I would urge, the historical study of the science in its development, and in its progressive adaptation to the circumstances of various nations. Under this would come questions relating to national and State policy, industrial, commercial, financial, educational, to the relations of capital to labor, and producers to distributors, to taxation, and a multitude of similar objects.

Next, I would name the study of what is generally classed as social science, including what pertains to the causes, prevention, alleviation, and cure of pauperism, insanity, crime, and various social difficulties. Nor would I neglect the study of the most noted theories and plans for the amelioration of society, the arguments in their support, the causes of their failure; and I would also have careful investigation into the relations of various bodies and classes which now apparently threaten each other. I would, for example, have the student examine the reasons why the communistic solution of the labor question has failed, and why the co-operative solution has succeeded.

As another subject of great importance, I would name the general principles of jurisprudence, and especially those principles which are more and more making their way in modern civilized nations. The advantage of this is evident; apart from the practical uses of such a study, who does not constantly feel in our general legislation too much of the attorney and too little of the jurist?

And in the study of general jurisprudence, I would urge the comparative and historical method. No country in the world affords so fine a field for such a method as our own. In all our States, political experiments are making; in all our legislatures, active-minded men are applying their solutions to the problems presented. The study of the comparative legislation of our own States, if supplemented by the study of the general legislation of other countries, could not fail to be of vast use in the improvement of society.

I would also have instruction given in the general principles of international law. In the development of this science lies much of happiness for the future of the world; but there is an important practical interest. Though the injunction of the Father of his Country to avoid entangling alliances has sunk deep into the American mind, there can be no doubt that before our country shall have attained a hundred millions of inhabitants, our diplomatic relations with other countries will require much more serious thought than now. It is not too soon to have this in view.

Happily, on all these subjects, and especially within the present century, a vast mass of precious experience and thought have been developed; many of the strongest men of the century have given their efforts to this; when Buckle says that Adam Smith, in his book, rendered to the world the greatest services that any one man has ever thus rendered, whether we agree with him or not as to the claim of his hero, we can hardly disagree as to the importance of the subject. There is something inspiring in this succession of great thinkers in these departments who have as their object the amelioration of society. Even to take the most recent of them, a line beginning with Adam Smith and continuing in our day with such men as Sismondi, Say, Stuart Mill, Roscher, Lieber, Woolsey, Carey, and Wells, can hardly fail to afford matter for study and thought.

In the thinking of such men, in the practice of the world as influenced by them, there is much to be learned; and if our country is to move forward with steadiness, or, indeed, if it is to lead in any particular direction, its statesmen must be more and more grounded in this thinking and practice.

Something should also be done in what is known in the European universities as "the science of administration" and "administrative law." The comparative study of statistics would come in here as a most important element. There is probably no legislator in the land—there is certainly no earnest student—who would not be greatly profited by a course of lectures based upon the tabulated statements, the graphic representations, and the maps of the last census report, so ably superintended by Professor Walker.

The question now arises as to the possibility of establishing a better provision for this advanced instruction. I fully believe that circumstances are most propitious, and for the following reasons:

First. The tendencies of large numbers of active-minded young men favor it. No observing professor in any college has failed to note the love of young Americans for the study and discussion of political questions; it constantly happens that students who evade ordinary scholastic duties, will labor hard to prepare themselves for such a discussion. So strong is this tendency that college authorities have often taken measures to check it; these measures have to a certain extent succeeded, yet I cannot but think that it is far better to direct such discussions than to check them. They seem to be a healthy outgrowth of our political life. Better, it seems to me, to send out one well-trained young man, sturdy in the town meeting, patriotic in the caucus, vigorous in the legislature, than a hundred of the gorgeous and gifted young cynics who lounge about city clubs, talk about "art" and "culture," and wonder why the country persists in going to the bad.

The second thing which augurs well for the promised reform, is the adaptability to it of our present university methods. Not many years since, it would have been almost impossible to make any adequate provision for these studies. Even in our foremost universities, the old collegiate system was dominant; each college had its single simple course, embracing a little Latin, Greek, and Mathematics, with a smattering of what were known as the physical, intellectual, and moral sciences.

At present the tendency is more and more toward *university* methods, toward the presentation of various courses, toward giving the student more freedom of choice among these. When carefully carried out, this has been found to yield admirable results; and the fact is now established that large numbers of young men, who under the old system confined rigidly to a single stereotyped course, would have wasted the greater part of their time, would have injured the quality of their minds by droning over their books, and injured their morals by slighting their duties, have become, when allowed to take courses more fitted to their tastes and aims, energetic students. The same reasons which have caused the creation of courses in our large universities, in which the principal studies are in the direction of philosophy, science, and modern literature, are valid for the creation of a course in which the studies shall relate to that science and literature most directly bearing upon public life.

I come now to the methods of such instruction, and would preface them by saying that, as regards our system of instruction at large in the public schools, it seems to me that more instruction should be given in general history, especially through political biography and in the history of our own country, as well as some training in the outlines of elements of political science; but on this I will not dwell. We are chiefly concerned now with the methods of this reform in *advanced* instruction in the higher preparation of those who are to instruct and lead in political and social matters.

Of these methods, I would name, first, a post-graduate course. In this there is one considerable advantage: students would come to it at ripe age and with considerable preliminary instruction. This advantage I do not underrate. No better use of funds could be made for our universities, or for the country, than in endowing post-graduate lectureships and fellowships in the main subjects involved. I would urge this method upon every man of wealth who wishes to leave a fame that will not rot with his body.

But valuable as this plan is, it has one great disadvantage— it is insufficient. The number of those who could afford the time and expense for such a course after an extended school and college and university training, and before a course of professional study, is comparatively small; besides this, we must take into account American impatience.

While, then, the plan of post-graduate courses would doubtless result in great good, it would fall far short of the work required. It would doubtless provide many valuable leaders in thought, but not enough to exercise the wide influence needed in such a nation as ours.

The second method, then, which I propose is the establishment in each of our most important colleges and universities of a full undergraduate course, which, while including studies in science and literature for general culture and discipline, shall have as its main subjects history, political and social science, and general jurisprudence.

A great advantage of this plan is the large number of students who would certainly profit by it.

I am convinced, by observation in four different colleges

and universities with which I have been connected as student and professor in our own country, and in several with which I have had more or less to do in foreign countries, that such a course, in any institution properly equipped, will attract large numbers of our most energetic young men, many of whom would not otherwise enter college at all; and that it would give forth a large body of graduates whose influence would be felt for good in all our States and Territories.

My proposal is that these studies, which are now mainly crowded into a few last months of the usual college course, be made the staple of an entire four years' course; that they be made a means of discipline, a means of culture, a means for the acquisition of profitable knowledge.

Objections will of course be urged; there will probably be none from any quarter against a post-graduate course; they will be entirely against the establishment of a full undergraduate course.

The first objection will doubtless be an appeal to conservatism. This must be expected from a multitude of excellent men, who generally look backward instead of forward; who think the past was on the whole good enough; who dislike change; who, when they have become accustomed to a system and fitted to it, instinctively dislike a new system, to which they may possibly find themselves not so well fitted. Their standing argument will be that the men who have achieved high political knowledge in spite of the present system, have done so by means of it.

A second and more precise objection will be on the score of discipline. Perhaps no word has been so unfortunate in American instruction as this; it has been made the fortress of every educational absurdity. In this particular case, we may ask why are not studies of political and social questions fully equal to any others in giving discipline? They call out our intellectual powers in discussing problems of the deepest human import; they bring into play our higher moral powers in judging between plans of institutions and lines of conduct on the plane of right and duty.

I claim for the studies in the course proposed an especial value in discipline. Any worthy discussion in political economy and social science gives valuable discipline for concentration and directness of mind; any proper discussion in history gives a discipline for breadth of mind; and these two sorts of discipline are fully equal to any given in any other courses of instruction.

It may also be objected, by men devoted to the physical sciences, that the powers of observation should be trained. In answer to this, it is sufficient to point out many men who in political studies have gained as great quickness in observation as can be found in any class of scientific men. It is hard to see that the observing powers of Montesquieu and John Stuart Mill and Francis Lieber were not as highly trained as those of Cuvier and Huxley and Agassiz.

The next objection will probably be on the score of culture. In this objection I see no force, because it is perfectly possible to bring studies for culture into the course proposed; nay, it is indispensable to bring in studies of at least one or two languages of the great modern states or their masterpieces in literature and art; while as to that culture which comes from a knowledge of nature it will not be difficult to give good instruction in scientific methods and results.

Again, it may be urged that young men are not mature enough and not sufficiently instructed to take up such studies on entering college. I answer, that it is not proposed to admit young men to these courses without reasonable preparation, nor is it proposed during the first year of such a course to plunge the student into the most difficult parts of it. He will be brought to these gradually by preliminary studies, properly combined with the subjects having as their aim general discipline and culture. The same objection could be made with equal force against any scientific course or any course in philosophy.

But granting that the objection has some force, the question is not what is ideally the best course, it is simply what is the best course possible; and experience shows that only undergraduate courses of the sort proposed will give any great number of the well-trained men we require. Against these objections should be constantly kept in view the main advantage, which is, the large number of students who would certainly take such a course.

But objections will be made on more general grounds.

The first may be called the optimist objection, that the people can be intrusted to enlighten themselves, that they are directly interested, and that self-interest is a most powerful stimulus; that the world has improved steadily, and will continue to do so. This is partly true. No one can deny that self-interest is a most powerful stimulus; but the point is to give more of that education which shall enable men to find out where their real self-interest is.

As to the fact that the world has improved steadily, I do not deny it, but simply observe that it is a question of cost; for few realize what a fearful price has been paid hitherto for the simplest advances in political and social science when achieved by the gradual growth of the popular mind. Take a few examples out of many.

Before England could learn what are to-day the simplest things in the proper adjustment of legislative and executive powers, the nation was dragged through a fearful civil war and through a long period of consequent demoralization: one king losing his head and another his crown. Before France, in the 17th century, could understand the simplest relations between her industrial policy and that of neighboring states; before she could realize that workmen on one side of a frontier are not necessarily the enemies of those on the other side, but rather helpers and co-workers, she was dragged through a series of wars which brought her to utter ruin; before, in the 18th century, she could learn what are now the axioms of political science applied to taxation, she had to go through a period of revolution, a period of anarchy, two periods of bankruptcy, two periods of despotism, with endless shedding of blood upon scaffolds and battle-fields and street-pavements. Before the world learned to accept the simplest modern axioms of toleration at the treaties of Passau and Westphalia, rivers of blood flowed through every great nation in Europe. Before the Prussian State could learn to allow political thinkers like Stein to work out the problem of her adjustment to modern ideas, she had to be crushed in battle, humbled in the dust by diplomacy, and to go through ten years of waste and war. Before the Austrian Empire could learn the principal relations of education to public policy, several generations had to be taught by military humiliations, and, among these Austerlitz, Magenta, and Sadowa. Before Italy could work out the problem of political unity, there came three hundred years of internal suffering; and possibly the future historian may point to a case hardly less striking on this side the Atlantic. Is it at least not worth an heroic effort to substitute a thorough education, reaching many of those who are to lead in public affairs, and so reaching the people themselves— an education in the observation of human experience and in reasoning upon it—in the hope that we may hereafter make progress at something less than the fearful price which the world has heretofore paid?

I confess that I am sanguine enough to hope that with more complete extension of political and social knowledge, with some training for better discussion of important political and social problems, the world may in the future begin to advance without paying the appalling cost for progress which she has paid and is still paying; but to bring this about, there must be effort; problems are arising at this moment before us as fearful as any that have ever disappeared behind us; the question between capital and labor alone is enough to exercise our best thought; it can easily give rise to scenes as fearful as any in human history. The question is whether such problems shall be solved by observant, patient, well-trained men, looking over large fields of human experience, applying to them the best human thought, or whether they shall be dealt with by declamation, passion, demagogism, trickery, nay, with the torch, the rifle, and the gallows.

Next comes the pessimist argument; it will be said "the greatest factor in republican development is personal force; the people will elect men of will-power, they will not elect your men of study and thought."

My answer is, first, that the effort in our proposed course is to lay hold on some of these men of personal force and will power, to bring them into the harness of real statesmanship rather than to leave them tethered by crotchets and half-truths.

But suppose all our men of study and thought are not elected, official positions are not the only means of influence; pen and tongue are often most powerful outside of official positions.

What we want is training for public service among men of various sorts of power; some in office, some in the press, some in the pulpit, some in the ordinary vocations of life.

In all these, we need men so trained that when a new question comes up, not only law-makers, but citizens in general, may be put in the way of right reasoning upon it; especially in times of excitement, or doubt, or distrust, do we need such men to lead the thinking of the community against political zealots or social desperadoes.

The time is surely coming, predicted in Macaulay's letter to Henry Randall—the time when disheartened populations will hear brilliant preaching subversive of the whole system of social order.

How shall this be met? Shall it be met by force? How by force where all is decided by majorities? Shall it be met by denunciation? Hardly; two can play at that, and while one side has the disadvantage of property to be destroyed, the other has the advantage of torches with which to destroy it. Shall it be met by revolution? As Danton said, "The revolution, like Saturn, destroys its own offspring." Shall it be met by Cæsarism? The first thing that Cæsar always does is to distribute bread and pageants to the mob, and rob the people to pay for them.

All these methods history shows to be futile; the only safeguard is in thorough provision for a regular, healthful, political development by the checking of popular unreason, and by the spreading of right reason; we must provide that when a brilliant lie is put forth, it shall be struck quickly and mortally, and before its venom has pervaded the social organism.

To do this we need men trained to grapple with political questions in every part of society. Shall we flatter ourselves that such gladiators in subversive thought as Proudhon, Carl Marx, Ferdinand Lasalle, and Bradlaugh can be met with platitudes? In the coming grapple with their apostles we shall find need of our best trained athletes. Can we trust to the subdivision of land in our country and the large number of small proprietors? So has it been in France for eighty years, and yet she has not escaped.

What we need is not talk, but discussion. Within the past few years we have seen the uses of such discussion; many of us have seen political and social heresies, some wild, some contemptible, put forth with force, with brilliancy, even at times with sincerity; in some quarters they have swept all before them; but wherever they have been met vigorously by men trained to grapple with them, they have been throttled, and the tide running in their favor has generally been turned.

If it be said that this has not constantly been the case, my reply is, that under our present system, we have no right to expect it; we cannot expect two or three men to breast the tide in a State containing millions of inhabitants, when such mistaken views are spreading like wild-fire; and yet, what has been done in some of our States by two or three men of force and thought, shows that if a small percentage of our college graduates had been as thoroughly instructed as these two or three, these heresies would have been met at the outset, and would never have attained dangerous proportions.

It may be objected that **such a system of** instruction would give us doctrinaires. Those who make this objection misread history; doctrinaires are **created** where theoretical politics are divorced from vigorous political life, where practical training and theoretical training are **not at** the same time present to modify each other. The French doctrinaires arose at a time when there was political discussion among a small knot of scholars, but no practical political life in the nation at large; the same thing was true until recently in Germany, and it has been true in Italy from **the days of** Machiavelli to the days of Cavour; it is true to-day in Russia; hence Nihilism, with all its miseries; but we look in vain for any perceptible influence of doctrinairism in England; there, political theory has never run away with leaders; it has been constantly modified by political **practice.** Edmund Burke was a close student of principles and theories, but who that has read his speech on American conciliation does not see that he justly claims to be a more practical statesman than any of his compeers, who trusted merely **to instinct** and what is called sound sense? Had Thomas Jefferson remained in France, he would doubtless have been a doctrinaire; as it was, we have in him a wonderful union of theoretical and practical training—Rousseau modified by the Virginia house of burgesses. The strength of the **great men who gave** this Republic its political foundation **lay in the** fact that no practical men ever studied theory and principles more thoroughly than they; Jefferson, Hamilton, John Adams, Jay, were close students of political principles and political history; Franklin and Washington, acute students of contemporary political history.

Besides this, the doctrinaires are by no means all **on the** theoretical side; there are not a few on the practical side. Our American life furnishes constant examples of this doctrinairism of practical men, quite **as** absurd as anything put forth by men of theory.

Moreover, in the system of instruction proposed, I would take effective means of preventing pedantry and doctrinairism by bringing in a constant circulation of healthful political thought from the outside. Much instruction should be given by lecturers holding their positions for short terms; these lecturers should be chosen, so far as possible, from men who take part in public life or business affairs practically, while not giving up the study of principles. The example cited in the first part of this report from European institutions will show that this plan is by no means impracticable.

Such will doubtless be the main objections to the plan proposed; they have been made in opposition to the same system in other countries, but the result has refuted them. As to the influence of a better system on this country, we should doubtless find it exercised first through the press. For the past ten years there has been a striking tendency observable among our most active young men toward the profession of journalism. The difference of feeling regarding such a career between the great body of students to-day and those of twenty years since is one of the curious things in the history of thought in this country.

The press would doubtless reveal the influence of this new education in quick, compact, thorough discussion of important subjects; it is not too much to hope that there would be much less declamation, defamation, and sensation writing, and much more vigorous reasoning.

We should doubtless next see this influence in the lower strata of public life. The young man who, on arriving from college and from his professional course, could supply really valuable information and make a straightforward argument upon living political and social questions in his town-meeting or board of supervisors, would take the first step in an honorable career. The character of our people is especially favorable to this; no people in the world so quickly recognize a man who can stimulate valuable thought; no country is so open to the influence of facts cogently presented. Even if men thus trained arrive sometimes at wrong conclusions, as doubtless they would, the habit of discussing questions with a more thorough knowledge and with closer reasoning could not fail to be of vast use; it would be found that political science, like other sciences, may be made to progress almost as much by mistaken reasoning, if it only be real, as by correct reasoning. Quesnay, Turgot, and the French physiocrats, by their errors as well as by their truths, stimulated Adam Smith, Ricardo, John Stuart Mill, and the English economists, and these in their turn, by their half truths as well as truths, stimulated List, Carey, Roscher, Wells, and the German and the American economists; the only thing that permanently hinders the growth of any science is dogmatism—the substitution of inherited opinions for thought, of accustomed inferences for real observation. Real thinking, however wrong some of its conclusions may **have been** temporarily, has always helped mankind in the long run.

Next, we should doubtless see the influence of such courses of instruction upon the legislative bodies of all **grades; even** our strong untutored men—men who rise by virtue of rough, uncultured native **force** and will-power—would feel strongly the influence of this instruction, even though they never came under it directly; better observations, better modes of thinking, better ideas would become common property; they would become an element in the political atmosphere, and the rude statesman of the future could not but feel its influence; thereby would he be stimulated to think more and orate less.

Nor should we forget the influence of such instruction upon the universities themselves; it would make them far greater **powers in** the formation of public opinion, therefore of far greater importance in public estimation. The present state of things is certainly not very encouraging to university officers; they know too well that their graduates have not taken that place in the conduct of public affairs which their education would seem to warrant; young men who have received so much greater advantages than others should, one would think, exercise much greater influence.

Unfortunately, statistics carefully collected show that the

relative number of college graduates in the executive and legislative positions of the country has been diminishing for many years. The main reason for this, is probably, that the majority of college students, under the present system, while obtaining their education, have been separated from the current of practical politics, and have not secured, to compensate for this separation, any education in theoretical politics; during four years in college, as well as four or five years' preparation for college, they have been studying matters often useful for culture, often important for discipline; but all this, so far as public influence is concerned, leaves them frequently at the first public meeting they attend, or the first public body in which they sit, inferior to many who have never enjoyed their advantages.

We have heard much of our educated men keeping aloof from politics; the examples of the older nations would lead us to believe that were scholarly young men trained steadily in political questions from the outset, they would enter public life at such an advantage that this charge would be brought to naught.

The good results of such courses as are now proposed would doubtless be speedily seen then, not only in the nation at large, but in the universities adopting them; such institutions could hardly fail to find their numbers increased; many young men, who do not go to college now, but who on leaving preparatory schools enter at once upon professional study, would think it worth their while to take a course embracing studies for which they have a taste, and fitting themselves for duties for which they have an ambition.

From every point of view, then, in the interest of individual students, many of whom would find scope for their powers, which they do not find in the existing courses, in the interests of the universities themselves, which might attract to their halls numbers of energetic young men, who now stand aloof from them; and above all, in the interest of State and national legislation—the example of our sister nations in establishing such courses is one which merits our close attention.

In looking over the whole field of education in the light of our own experience and that of other nations, I see no better object for the earnest efforts of those called upon to administer our greater institutions for advanced education. I am well aware that few, if any, have means enough, even for the present courses; it is then a case for the exercise of American munificence; here there is reason to hope for much. In the Old World, with its systems of primogeniture and its means of entailing fortunes, men of great wealth can found families and hand their property down to remote generations. So it is not in our own land; the great fortune of the first generation rarely lasts farther than the third. While, then, some reason exists there for hoarding enormous sums for heirs, here there is none, and to this fact are doubtless due many acts of munificence which have honored the American name, and blessed the country. Let us hope that it will not be the ambition of our wealthy men to become **the fatty tumors of society**—abnormal growths—accumulating fortunes which are at best, only to be reäbsorbed into the ordinary business channels; but that they will see the duty and the honor lying before them; that in making provision for the higher education of their fellow-citizens, and especially in those branches which insure better government and a higher type of citizenship, they will rear to themselves monuments more lasting than statues of bronze or obelisks of granite; on such imperishable monuments already stand the names of Harvard, Yale, Smithson, Peabody, Cooper, Packer, Johns Hopkins, Cornell, Vassar, Sage, Wells, McGraw, Sibley, and their noble compeers. Let us hope that worthy successors of these may arise to provide, upon the foundations already laid by our stronger universities and colleges, means for an instruction worthy of our land, in history, political and social science, and general jurisprudence—in all that directly fits and strengthens men to advance the nation by taking part in public affairs.

MODERN HISTORY AT OXFORD.

The following chapter, by Mr. W. J. Ashley, M. A., Fellow and Tutor of Lincoln College at Oxford, written for that interesting and instructive volume on "Oxford: Its Life and Schools,"[1] edited by A. M. M. Stedman, M. A., of Wadham College, assisted by members of the University of Oxford, is reprinted in this connection for the sake of showing the present status of history and political science in that institution. The chapter admirably complements the earlier notes and observations of Professor Paul Fredericq, of the University of Ghent, upon the Study of History in England and Scotland, recently published as No. 10, of our Fifth Series.

"The Honour School of Modern History has itself a history which covers some four-and-thirty years. A School of 'Law and Modern History' was one of the results of that reforming movement which led to the first University Commission. For twenty years these subjects were yoked together, until in 1872 two independent Schools were established; while the present regulations came into force as lately as 1886. In spite of

---

[1] Oxford: Its Life and Schools. London: George Bell and Sons, York Street, Covent Garden, 1887. This convenient and readable book of 359 pages will prove serviceable to students of English educational history. The work contains a brief historical sketch of the University of Oxford and of its various colleges. Student expenses at Oxford; its social, intellectual, and religious life; its system of examinations; its pass schools and various departments of study are all concisely described. There are also interesting accounts of Women's Education at Oxford and of the novel system of University Extension, recently mentioned in the *Studies*, No. 11, Fifth Series.

many difficulties, to which it were not surprising had the School succumbed, it has steadily grown in importance. The work has become more thorough, the teaching better organized, the examination standard higher; and now the study of Modern History excites so keen an interest and gives an intellectual stimulus to so many that it must be reckoned one of the most powerful forces in Oxford life.

"Before speaking of the considerations which may lead a man to choose this particular School, let us see what work it sets before him. In the first place, he is required to study the outlines of the whole of English History, both political and constitutional; then, secondly, he is to give special attention to a 'Period' of both English and Foreign History,—thus, should he select the Period of Foreign History from 1414 to 1610, he must take the Period of English History from 1399 to 1603. He will, in addition, be examined in Political Science, and in Economic History and Theory. And, finally, those who aim at a good class are required to offer also a Special Subject, with certain specified 'original authorities.'

"Now the first and most difficult point to be settled by the man who begins to read Modern History is, which Period he shall 'take.' The Periods are, roughly, as follows: (1) from the fifth to the eleventh century; (2) the ninth to the thirteenth; (3) the thirteenth to the fifteenth; (4) the fifteenth and sixteenth; (5) the seventeenth; (6) the eighteenth; (7) from the middle of last century to the middle of this. The selection will of course be determined largely by individual preferences; one man may wish to examine mediæval society, another the great changes accompanying the Renaissance and Reformation, while a third may be more interested in the politics of the age immediately preceding our own: but with most the choice will be also influenced by regard to the Special Subjects. Of these six are mentioned in the regulations, viz., Hildebrand, the first three Crusades, Italy (1492–1513), the Great Rebellion (1638–1649), the French Revolution (1789–1795), and India (1773–1805); and although Candidates are permitted to offer other subjects, after giving due notice and obtaining the approval of the Board of Faculty, the fact that only in these six are they likely to obtain assistance from tutors and lectures is practically sure to restrict them to those suggested. It will clearly be wise to choose such a Period and such a Special Subject that the latter may fall within the former. With some men it will be the General Period that will determine the Special Subject, but with most the reverse will be the case. Let us assume, then, that the first point to be decided is, which Special Subject to study. Each has its own interest and attraction. The first will give some insight into the character and work of the mediæval Church, and its relations to the Empire and the secular power; the second shows Christendom and Mahometanism in conflict; the third, the Renaissance and the death of the Italian Republics; the fourth, the struggle between Charles and the English Parliament; the fifth, the overthrow of the *ancien régime* in France; the sixth, the creation of our Indian Empire. In the first and the second, again, the original authorities with which the student will have to deal are in Latin, those for the third in French and Italian, for the fifth in French only, and for the fourth and sixth in English only.

"One more alternative is presented. A candidate, instead of choosing a historical Special Subject, may offer himself to be examined in the History of the Law of Real Property, and in this case he will not be influenced by his Special Subject in the choice of a Period. 'Real Property' has the advantage of lying in a comparatively narrow compass; and this may induce those to take it up who shrink from handling the masses of original authorities which the other special subjects put before them. Men interested in modern land-questions may feel themselves drawn to the 'Real Property' as likely to be of practical value; while those who intend to become barristers or solicitors may see in it a convenient introduction to their more strictly professional studies. On the other hand the subject is very technical, and but loosely connected with the other work of the School; and it certainly seems unwise for a man who has gained a general knowledge of a Period not to try to add to it that insight into character, that training of judgment and sympathy to which the detailed study of a historical Special Subject may help him.

"We will suppose then that, having considered the relation of Special Subject to General Period, a man has made up his mind which Subject and Period he will take. And matters have not been unduly anticipated, in thus first directing attention to the General Period and the Foreign History; for, although tutorial help on the Foreign History is usually deferred until the third term or even the second year of reading, it is necessary to attend lectures upon it from the first, if the ground is to be covered in the time. Supposing a man to know something of general English History, and to have two years before him, he may do well to assign his time thus,—the first long vacation and the two following terms to English Constitutional and Political History; the next term, long vacation, and another term, to the General Period, English and Foreign, a term to the Special Subject, and the last term to Political Science and Economic History.

"English Constitutional History is the backbone of the School: around it may be grouped all that it is really necessary to know of what is oddly called 'Political' History; and it gives a strength and dignity to the School which it might otherwise lack. But Constitutional History means the study of Stubbs and Hallam,—books which appal the beginner, and of which the former will, not improbably, somewhat bewilder him. The student, when he plunges into it, seems to enter a forest of *gesiths* and *gemots*, of assizes and *justiciars*, of *tenths* and *fifteenths*, where the paths all run into another, and lead nowhither. And, therefore, it may be found more profitable for him, before attacking his Stubbs and Hallam, to go through a little preliminary course of reading; so that when he comes to the greater works he may understand what sort of questions he has to deal with, what are the points at issue, 'what it is all driving at.' Let him therefore commence with Professor Freeman's 'Growth of the English Constitution;' then let him look at the working of our political institutions to-day, as explained, for instance, in the chapters on the Cabinet and the House of Commons in Bagehot's 'English Constitution,' and in the first two lectures of Professor Dicey's 'Law of the Constitution.' Then, turning back, let him carefully analyse the 'Introduction' to Stubbs' 'Select Charters,' where every word is worthy of letters of gold. And now he will be in a fit state to open the Bishop of Chester's great work, with some confidence in his power to see the significance of its statements and generalizations.

"It would be impossible here to go through the list of General Periods and Special Subjects, and give suggestions on each of them. But something perhaps may be said of what is meant by Political Science and Economic History. The Political Science paper differs from the rest, in that it is not set upon a certain limited subject-matter, though, indeed, definite books are mentioned. It is expected that, whatever Period a man studies, his work will make him think of the political principles for which men then strove, and their relation to the principles of to-day, of the strength and action of political forces then and now; and that he will come to the reading of the prescribed books with some knowledge of the significance of the subjects of which they treat.

"The authors chosen are Aristotle, Hobbes, Maine, and Bluntschli, and it may be well to explain why these have been selected. Aristotle's 'Politics' is by far the most important of all writings on Political Philosophy. It is the first systematic treatise dealing with the great questions of social organization, and it has permanently affected the language of political theory. But it is of special value to the student of History. For it gives the theory of the ancient state, and by the very contrasts which it suggests, above all by its limitations and omissions, helps us to see wherein the mediæval and modern world alike differ from the ancient.

"Yet the mediæval world has this in common with the ancient, that in both the interests of the individual were held to be subordinate to the interests of the State. But in the sixteenth century another conception of the State began to influence men, one which regarded individuals as having certain rights independent of any social union, and as having created the State for certain limited objects. This theory that the State originated in, or rested on, a contract between individuals, underlay, in the shape given to it by Locke, the Whig doctrine of parliamentary sovereignty; and, as taught by Rousseau, was held to justify the claim to rebellion as a right. But it was Hobbes who first consistently and powerfully worked out the theory; and it can be all the more calmly considered on its own merits when it is presented by Hobbes as a support to authority, and not as a weapon against it.

"Maine's 'Ancient Law' is also in its measure a typical and representative work; for it marks the beginning in England of the application of the 'historical method' to political and social institutions. The history of the growth of an institution does not always explain its value; but it may at any rate show that many an idea which we are accustomed to regard as necessary and self-explanatory, is itself the result of a long development. And, finally, the student is directed to Bluntschli's 'Theory of the State,' as a useful book of reference; . . . . . .

"Men are, however, usually more afraid of the Political Economy paper than of that on Political Science. The regulations set forth that they 'will be examined in Mill's Political Economy,' and 'will also be required to show an adequate knowledge of Economic History.' But if they plunge into Mill they find the greater part of his book extremely difficult, and, what is more important, out of relation to the rest of their reading. Besides, they can scarcely fail to learn that Mill's conclusions have been largely modified by subsequent economists, and they will naturally ask, whether they are expected to follow the discussions through the writings of

Jevons and Cairnes and Sidgwick. On the other hand, Economic History is by itself a wide subject, and a subject for which there are no good text-books. The fact is that a great change is coming over the character of economic teaching in England, and the regulations of the History School are probably only transitional. For the present most investigators of Economic History would agree in thus defining their attitude toward orthodox Economics: they do not deny that the teaching of Ricardo and Mill is a logical construction upon given assumptions, nor that these assumptions are in a large measure true of certain important sides of modern industrial life, but they assert that these assumptions were certainly not at all true until very recent times. And, therefore, they urge, the so-called 'principles' of Political Economy are, at any rate, not universally true for all times and places, and, in consequence, contribute scarcely at all to the understanding of the economic life of the past. For this it is necessary to study economic institutions in the light of the ideas of the time, and to examine those ideas, not in relation to modern conditions which did not then exist, but in relation to the conditions amid which they rose. What, therefore, is desired in the History School is probably this, that men should gain some sort of acquaintance with the chief features of the development of English Industry, Agriculture and Commerce, and with the ideas influencing and underlying it; and therefore, that they should also know the chief doctrines of modern economists, without which the social history of the last hundred years is scarcely intelligible. But it is to Economic History rather than to modern Theory that attention is chiefly to be directed. The following reading may be suggested,

"Cunningham, 'English Industry and Commerce,' Book I., chaps. i., ii.; Books II., III., IV.; Rogers, 'Work and Wages,' chaps. ii.–vi., viii.–xii., xiv.–xx.; Toynbee, 'Industrial Revolution of 18th Century,' lectures ii.–v., vii.–x. The last-named writer's essay on 'Ricardo and the old Political Economy,' will explain the assumptions common to Mill and all the great English Economists. Then it will save time and trouble to run rapidly through some short treatise, such as Jevons' 'Primer,' so as to gain familiarity with modern terms. After this one may address oneself to Mill, and read with especial care, Book I., chaps. x.–xii.; Book II., chaps. vi.–xvi.; Book III., chaps. i.–iv., x., xiii., xvii., xxiv.; Book IV., chap. vii.; Book V., chaps. ii.–iv., vii., xi.

"As to the reading necessary for the Periods and Special Subjects, reference should be made to the lists of books in the Examination Statutes, and it would be scarcely possible to make here any detailed suggestions. But some words as to the general character of the work may not be out of place.

"The work is of three kinds: attendance at lectures, reading, essay-writing. And in the History School, essay-writing has become the usual way of 'doing work for one's tutor.' Men are advised at the beginning of the term to give special attention to some particular Period, certain books are suggested, and 'subjects' falling within their reading are 'set' for essays. Now, why has this particular method been adopted?

"For boys at school there is probably no better way of teaching than to cause them to learn the main facts in such a way that they can remember them. But in the study of History in the University the learning of bare facts is the smallest, and in a sense the least important, part of the work. By going to the usual authorities, any tolerably industrious man can readily find a sufficient number of facts,—of dates and events. What he really wants to know is the meaning of these facts, what stages they mark in the growth of such and such an institution, what policy they show in the action of a particular statesman, what contrasts they suggest between different ages and nations. And essay-writing seems the best way to develop this habit of looking for causes and effects. Let the student first quietly read the necessary authorities upon the subject, making as he does so a rough abstract of what they contain; then let him jot down his ideas, in some dozen words, and make up his mind what his line of argument is going to be, what he is going to say first and next, and how he is going to end; and then, *when he sees to the end* of what he is going to say, and not before, let him begin. The salvation of an essay is 'point.'

"Now of course this, like all other conceivable methods, has its risks. It dangerously encourages fine writing; it may make a man undervalue reading and investigation in comparison with facility in constructing neat arguments. Yet, under the criticism of a tutor, it is the best way of making the reading for the History School a really valuable mental discipline. For, as Professor Seeley has so admirably said, 'in History everything depends on turning narrative into problems. So long as you think of History as a mere chronological narrative, so long you are in the old literary groove which leads to no trustworthy knowledge, but only to that pompous conventional romancing, of which all serious men are tired. Break the drowsy spell of narrative; ask yourself questions; set yourself problems; your mind will at once take up a new attitude; you will cease to be solemn and begin to be serious.'

"Nor is it as unnecessary as it ought to be to insist on the importance of impartiality. No such opportunity will ever come again of forming right judgments, and it were a pity to lose all the benefit that could be gained, because of previously created bias. This does not mean that a man is to get rid of all his opinions beforehand, or that he should not hope to retain those he has. He may fairly think Strafford a hero, and Cromwell a hypocrite, or Cromwell a saviour of liberty, and Strafford a tool of despotism; and he may fairly hope that the result of his reading will be to confirm him in these opinions. But this need not cause him always to take for granted that the one was wrong or the other right. Let him try to be scrupulously fair, and to think how the matter presented itself to the actor himself.

"What is necessary in dealing with individuals is still more necessary in dealing with institutions. Be ready to recognize that a great organization had *some* value for its own time. It will be a great help towards clearness of perception if question-begging terms are scrupulously avoided; thus, even if a man thinks that the mediæval papacy was a curse to the world, he will not be giving up any principle if he speaks of its 'claims,' instead of its 'pretensions.'

"Perhaps, at this point, we are in a position to answer the question: Why should a man read for the History School? Because, in the first place, it is in many cases a peculiarly valuable preparation for after life. Suppose, for instance, that a man intends to take Holy Orders. Theology is a study which, more than any other, requires a combination of powers, —the power to understand and sympathize with high feeling and emotion, the power on the other hand of estimating at its true value the 'practical side' of life. And in each direction, History will help him. It will give him, moreover, a wider horizon; he will learn something of the relation of the Church to Society and the State; he will see how men, in other times and conditions, have dealt with the problems with which he also has to deal.

"Or again, suppose he intends to enter 'business.' There is no danger so great to the business man as the danger of being immersed in the present, of caring only for the immediate circumstances of the immediate occupation. For such a man it will be a great safeguard to have made acquaintance with other motives and forces than those which he is likely to meet in business, to be able to appreciate forms of society very different from those in which he is placed, to understand how much the world has changed in the past, and, therefore, how much it may change in the future.

"Again, does not the History School offer an excellent training for the politician or journalist? The business of politics is becoming increasingly difficult; it demands, above all, knowledge and seriousness. Only by studying the past can the necessary knowledge be gained, and nothing is so likely to impress a man with the tremendous importance of the issues which the pettinesses of party warfare conceal.

"But the History School would not be so highly valued as it deserves, were it only regarded as suitable to men who look forward to certain particular professions. Of course, like any other mental discipline, it teaches industry and method; but its peculiar value lies rather in the training of the *judgment*. It may make us discover the good in some cause or movement which yet we may feel it our duty to oppose; may make us see the long past causes of present evils, and the far future results of action now lightly begun; and it may encourage the habit of suspension of judgment till the judgment has sufficient materials to build upon."

RECENT IMPRESSIONS OF THE ÉCOLE LIBRE.

The following letter, addressed to the Editor by one of his advanced students, Mr. T. K. Worthington,[1] who, after pursuing the three years' graduate course in history and politics at the Johns Hopkins University, went to Paris upon a university appointment for further study in historical and political science before taking his Doctor's degree in Baltimore. This communication, of course, embodies only first impressions; but they are altogether favorable to the Parisian School of Politics, and supplement President White's earlier observations. They are, moreover, confirmed by impressions communicated orally to the Editor by Dr. Frederic A. Bancroft, a graduate of the Columbia College School of Political Science, who has studied at the École Libre des Sciences Politiques for a considerable period, as well as in Berlin and at Freiburg with Dr. H. von Holst. While deeply and gratefully appreciating the advantages of graduate study at German universities, the Editor strongly believes that many of his countrymen make a serious mistake in not spending at least a portion of their graduate study in Europe in one of the schools of Paris. In form and methods of presentation, in lucidity of style and logical directness of statement, in the adaptation of scientific means to practical

---

[1] Mr. Worthington is the author of the Historical Sketch of the Finances of Pennsylvania, published by the American Economic Association, vol. II. No. 2. 85 pp., 1887.

ends, the French are good masters, and in the substance of historical and political knowledge they are richer to-day than ever before. Men who can afford to do so ought to combine the best that France, Germany, England and America have to teach in the line of methods and special literature in their chosen branches of history and politics, and to make the resultant culture connect with the academic, civic, economic or political needs of our own country. The whole weight of college and university influence in America ought to be thrown into higher education in history and politics for the sake of promoting good citizenship, elevating public opinion, and improving American administration—local, State and national.

PARIS, *December* 1, 1887.

Your letter of November 3, asking me to give you my impressions of the advantages which Paris offers as regards instruction in Political Science, has been received and duly considered. It is impossible so early in the academic year to commit myself to anything more than first impressions, but to these you are more than welcome.

The lectures at the École Libre des Sciences Politiques began on the 14th of November, but no other courses of any importance will be open until the middle of December. If one may judge from the official programmes there are a great many opportunities to hear valuable and interesting lectures on subjects directly and indirectly connected with political science. As soon as I was comfortably settled in lodgings, I procured M. Fourneau's "Programme des Cours publics de Paris" and "Le Livret de l'Étudiant de Paris," from which, with the programme of the École Libre, may be gathered exact information as regards all the courses to be given during the coming year.

Leaving the École Libre out of consideration for a moment, I shall attempt to give a brief account of the announcements so far as they have been made up to the present time. The Faculté de Droit, the Faculté des Lettres, the École pratique des Hautes Études, the Collége de France, the **Institut National** Agronomique, the École des Ponts et Chaussées, the Conservatoire National des Arts et Métiers, the École Nationale des Chartes, and the École d'Anthropologie, have announced twenty-three courses (thirty-seven hours a week) **on** subjects which may fairly be covered by the term "Political Science." This seems to afford a large field for selection, but it is **one which is** soon limited by close inspection. The courses at the technical schools consist mostly of elementary lectures on political economy. At such institutions as the École National Agronomique, the École des Ponts et Chaussées, and the Conservatoire National des Arts et Métiers, the courses **are almost** entirely supplementary to some particular phase of technology. At the last named the second year of study is devoted to Diplomacy, History **of** Political Institutions, and Administration, the Sources of French History, and the Classification of Archives: one lecture a week on each subject. None of the **above-named** schools would be of much value to the general **student of** political science. The courses in law, on the other hand, are too special for the average American, unless he wishes to go deeply into the study of Roman Law. In this case the advantages are very great. Fifty lectures a week will be given by the Faculté de Droit, most of which are closely connected with the study of Roman Law. At the École pratique des Hautes Études there will not be a single course this year in political science. There is a course of one hour a week at the École d'Anthropologie on the History of Civilization, which might prove interesting. **In** the programme of the Faculté des Lettres I came upon a welcome announcement: M. Fustel de Coulanges is booked for two hours a week on the Institutional History of the Middle Ages. As the course does not open for two weeks I am compelled to postpone my impressions of M. de Coulanges as a lecturer. M. Pigonneau is down for a course of two hours **a** week on the History of French Diplomacy under Richelieu. **M.** Pigonneau is lecturing with great success at the École Libre, on the Diplomatic History of Europe from 1648 to 1789. He is followed by about 90 auditors. There is also a lecture once a week by M. Lavisse on the History of the Prussian State from 1648 to 1815.

At the College de France, M. Paul Leroy-Beaulieu will give two hours a week on Political Economy; M. Flach, two a week on the History of Comparative Legislation; M. Joly, two a week on the Law of Nature, and the Law of Nations; M. Levasseur, one a week on Historical Geography and Economic Statistics. It appears, therefore, that the choice lies between the College de France, and the Faculté des Lettres. Whatever I do this winter, I expect to hear MM. Fustel de Coulanges and Leroy-Beaulieu.

You are doubtless anxious to hear something about the École Libre des Sciences Politiques. As you know, it is an institution whose aim it is to give advanced and special instruction in political science. That it meets a need in the community may be emphasized by the statement that it was founded in 1871, and that it opens the present academic year with about 500 students on the rolls. It is very difficult to get information as regards the number of students, the number of books in the library, the financial situation of the institution, and such matters, which are more freely discussed in America. Before going any further, I should like to give you a brief account of the origin of the school.

The École Libre is the result of private enterprise. It is a joint stock company with a moderate amount of capital, all of which is paid up. The institution was founded in 1871, and the first courses were opened January 10, 1872—a red-letter day in the history of practical education. At the start, the resources of the school were exceedingly moderate. Scarcely fifty shares of the stock had been taken. The only resources were several thousand francs, collected by the director of the school, as endowments for certain chairs, and various amounts advanced by the *comité de fondation*.

The founders of this great institution, when they trace its history back to 1871, realize the magnitude of the task which they had set before them. They had very small means, they were at the mercy of the government, inexperienced, with a hostile public to oppose them. No one believed that they could succeed in an undertaking which seemed to need all the power of the state to back it, or that they could keep aloof from the strife of political parties. Such an experiment, without doubt, needed the greatest caution.

The school opened in very humble style. A single room was rented, in which five lecturers delivered each a course of twenty-five lectures. The first students were apathetic: they had "*la physionomie de simples curieux.*" For the most part they took no notes. Success followed close upon the opening of the door of the humble lecture-room. MM. Janet and Levasseur gave the school a certain prestige. M. Sorel at once excited attention by his admirable lectures on diplomacy, and M. Paul Leroy-Beaulieu, already well known as a publicist, soon acquired an equal reputation as a lecturer on political economy and finance. In the selection of this staff, the directors were influenced by no party consideration whatever. This has been the key-note of the history of the institution: in this sense alone is it a "free school." Within five months after the first lecture was delivered, all the capital was subscribed, and the management was put in possession of a considerable fund. The field of action was at once enlarged, and in the fall of 1872 the school was moved to more commodious quarters in the rue Taranne.

The first plan of instruction was found to be defective in two ways. First (in M. Boutmy's own words), lectures which covered so much ground and were delivered "du haut de la chaire" could not embody much analysis of detail. They kept out of sight the method pursued by the professor in reaching his conclusion: his rules of criticism and research. "L'Élève est transporté tout d'abord au point d'arivée, il ne connaît rien de la route parcourue. Il n'est capable ni de la parcourir à son tour, ni de prendre exemple de ce qu'il a vu faire pour trouver sa voie dans des études du même genre." The directors recognized the advantages of the seminary-method.

Secondly, they found that, unless their institution had some object beyond the completion of a liberal education, they would be compelled to close their doors for want of students. They found that young Frenchmen were devoting less and less time to the interval between completing their collegiate studies and their entrance into business or professional life.

These considerations dictated the arrangement of the new plan. In the first place, the teaching force was increased and the ground which each lecturer covered was limited and better defined. In the second place, the *conférence* or *seminar* was introduced. The seminary system has been a great feature in the instruction of the École Libre. M. Boutmy defines the *conférence* as "an informal lecture, where the professor and students meet around the same table to handle documents (a budget, a file of diplomatic papers, or a statistical table—as the case may be), to comment upon texts, to study statistics, to discuss and settle points of difference, and to clear up all obscurities by means of their united efforts. The object of the *conférence* is not less important than that of the formal lecture. It is to exercise the understanding, to cultivate certain faculties which the *ex cathedra* instruction fails to develop, to give the student access to original sources and to teach their critical use." By referring to the programme of the École Libre, which I sent you some time ago, you may easily see how great a part the *conférence* plays in the course of instruction for the coming year. There are sixteen lectures and eleven *conférences* a week. In seven cases the *maître de conférences* holds a government office.

The *conférences* are divided according to subjects as follows:—Finance and financial administration, 4; diplomacy and diplomatic history, 2; international law, 1; money banking, etc., 1; colonial geography, 1; France in North Africa,

1. As I said above, it appeared at the beginning that if the school was to be a success it **must** have a practical end in view: the managers, accordingly organized the courses in such a way, that they might be able to offer candidates for certain branches of government service, a thorough preparation for the duties of their respective departments. It is to serve this end that practical administrators are chosen as *maîtres de conférences*. The candidates of the École Libre have always been the most successful in the state examinations. From 1876 to 1886, out of 60 men who passed the examinations for the *Conseil d'État*, 47 (78 per cent.) were prepared by the École Libre. Out of 46 who passed the examinations **for the** Inspection des Finances, during the same period, **41** (89 per cent.) were prepared by the École Libre. Since 1880, **all the** successful candidates in this department, were prepared by the school.

In the examinations for the **Cour des** Comptes held **in** 1879, 1882, 1884 and **1886,** the men trained at the École Libre obtained sixteen places out of seventeen. During the last few years all candidates prepared by the school for the ministry of foreign affairs have been admitted to the highest places. In 1886, out of eleven candidates received into this department, nine, who stood highest, belonged to the École Libre.

These are the practical results. Each year witnesses some addition to the advantages offered to candidates for the State examinations. If time and space permitted, it would be interesting to trace the growth of the practical tendency by comparing the curriculum during the early years of the school with the announcements made for the coming year. The organization has changed somewhat since 1872. At that time the whole system of instruction was grouped under two sections: (1) Administration and Finance. (2) Diplomacy. In the programme for this year the courses are classified as follows: Diplomatic Section, Administrative Section, Economic and Financial Section, Colonial Section, General Section, Public Law and History. These correspond to the following departments of the government service: Diplomacy, Conseil d'État, Administration, Inspection des Finances, Cour des Comptes and the Colonial Service. Such courses as do connect directly with these branches form a valuable preparation for business and commercial life, or "le couronnement naturel de toute éducation libérale." I know a Frenchman from the South who is taking the courses in finance, in order to prepare himself for a position in his father's bank.

The progress of the school may be illustrated by the increase in the number of students:

1871–72	89
1873–74	96
1874–75	150
1876–77	191
1878–79	222
1887–88	500

This is a remarkable record. Such an institution as this we must have some day in Baltimore or in our national capital. When the time comes to make the experiment, the experience of the École Libre will be invaluable.

Before closing this over-long communication, I must say a few words about the impressions gained from my short experience. The building occupied by the École Libre is at 27 Rue St. Guillaume, a few steps from the Boulevard St. Germain. It is about fifteen minutes' walk from the Place de la Concorde, and easily accessible by 'bus and tram. On entering the building you pass through a small ante-room, with the office of the *concièrge* on the left, and come into a large cloak-room. To the left of the cloak-room is a large room with a glass roof, where the men walk, smoke and talk between the lectures. At one end of the promenade is the lavatory, and at the other, across a passage, are the offices of the director and secretary. The amphitheatre is at the end of the passage, which also opens on the cloak-room. All the lectures are delivered in the Salle de Cours, which is entered from the recreation hall. This room is furnished with eight baize-covered tables, each about a yard wide and seating ten men. The chairs around the walls accommodate twenty or thirty more. Sometimes the room is uncomfortably crowded and very hot, though the average attendance is about ninety. The lecturer's desk is at one end of the room on a platform. There are no windows but a glass roof, consequently there are no cross lights.

Up stairs, in the rear, are three library rooms containing, I should say, about 8,000 volumes. There are three library funds belonging: (1) to the school, (2) to the société d'Enseignement supérieur, (3) to the société de linguistique. In the second story front are two journal rooms containing about 100 foreign and French reviews and the daily papers. The building is exceedingly comfortable. A large addition is being erected which will give greatly increased accommodations.

The lectures are very formal. The professor is ushered into the hall by the concièrge, who conducts him with great ceremony to the platform, takes his hat and coat and retires. On the table is a small waiter holding a tumbler, a carafe of water and a bowl of sugar. From these ingredients the professor compounds a drink, which must be singularly unexhilarating, takes a sip thereof, and the lecture begins. To an American, accustomed to a less pretentious début on the part of his professor, the above performance gives an unexpressible sense of éclat. The lecturer and the auditors evidently consider the lecture to be the event of the day. Nearly all my lectures are at four o'clock in the afternoon. Professor and students, almost to a man, appear in high hat, black coat, and gloves. The happy possessor of an eye-glass sports it. All this is very pleasant, though it is objected to by some Americans as incompatible with good scholarship.

I had heard a great deal against French lectures. Those at the École Libre are open to little criticism. They are like the audience and the professor—formal, highly polished and well got up. The lecturer has his subject thoroughly worked out. He knows exactly what part of the ground he will cover at each lecture, and we stay until he covers it, if it takes an hour and a half. Each lecture, as a rule, begins with a a short review of the previous one, and ends with a brief résumé of the points just gone over. The greatest care is given to style and literary finish. So far from being sketchy and superficial, the lectures are sometimes overloaded with detail. The historical treatment of a subject is very full and closely connected.

Much stress should be laid on the difference in method between the formal lecture and the *conférence*. The extreme formality and solemnity of the *cours* marks the distinction. No time is lost in questions put to the lecturer and all discussion is reserved for the *conférence*. My greatest objection is that no bibliography is given by the lecturer. If I did not happen to have some knowledge of the books on finance and administration, I should be entirely in the dark as regards reading.

The men take very careful notes. I have seen a man's notes on one lecture amount to twelve closely-written pages. The charge of superficiality cannot be made against the lecturers at the École Libre. Superficiality is almost impossible. The professors, as a rule, are men of affairs—either practical administrators or prominent in politics. They are forced, by their training and by the plan of the institution, to be thorough. The administrative and financial sections employ five lecturers. Four of them hold positions under the government. Many of the faculty embody what I have always thought to be a charming combination—the scholar and the man of the world.

I said that the lectures were not superficial. I must make an exception. When the lecturer comes to treat of the United States, he is apt to give an American a bad impression of his scholarship. In certain cases, where the syllabus led me to expect an interesting comparative or historical study of English or American institutions, I met with grievous disappointments. The remarks made on such occasions were generally absurd, and **threw** no light on the matter under discussion. At first, ignorance of America on the part of European scholars distressed me a great deal. Last year, at Oxford, Professor Dicey was pointed out to me by a lecturer on constitutional history as a curiosity—almost a monstrosity—because he was the only man in Oxford who knew anything about the Constitution of the United States.

If **anyone** should ask me whether it would be profitable for an American to spend a portion of his period of Continental study in Paris, I should say emphatically, **yes**. I cannot conceive of an institution which could offer greater advantages than the École Libre to the student of **political science**. The fact that it is, in great part, a primary school for **the government** makes it less valuable to the foreigner than it otherwise might be. It should be clearly understood, however, that it is not the purpose of the directors to make the École Libre solely a preparatory school for the civil service. On the contrary, it is their ideal to make the institution a great University of Political Science. Where the civil service examinations are so universal as they are in France, such a **university** would always have necessarily a practical side. There are many courses at the École Libre, which have a purely educational or non-utilitarian value.

There are many points which I have omitted. I have not touched upon the subject of examinations as I have had no experience of them. You are well acquainted with the Annales d l'École Libre des Sciences Politiques. I remember that it is on the seminary table in the Bluntschli Library. An interesting feature is the *groupes de travail*. These are seminaries of the alumni, held under the direction of members of the faculty. Three groups are organized: (1) Finance, (2) Public and private law, (3) History and diplomacy. There is also an association of the alumni. Every five years a travelling fellowship is awarded to graduates of certain standing.

The value is 5,000 francs. There are various prizes distributed each year among the graduating class. Their total value is 1,200 francs.

M. Boutmy has been most kind and helpful in every way. Later in the winter I hope I shall be able to give you more extensive and trustworthy impressions than these which I herewith submit.

PREPARATION FOR THE CIVIL SERVICE IN GERMAN STATES.[1]

The purpose of the following paper is to give a short report of the laws which at present regulate the course preparing for the qualified service of the German states. Germany has so long been known as the country of model administration, her system is so perfectly developed in all its ramifications that the student of political science will always with interest and pride look upon this masterpiece of political praxis. And he has a right to feel proud, for the successes of the statesmen merely followed the triumphs of German theory. All the great reforms, from the administrative reform of Stein to the social reform of Bismarck, would have never been achieved by men who were not thoroughly educated in political science. For this reason we shall direct attention to the German system of political education, which is the motive power of the political machine. Our authority is the XXXIV publication of the "Verein für Socialpolitik."

BAVARIA.

The regulations concerning the examination for the civil service were issued in 1830; at that time the administrative and judicial departments were not yet completely separated, and consequently the study and examination qualifying for

---

[1] The above article was prepared by Mr. L. Katzenstein, of the Johns Hopkins University, formerly of the University of Berlin.—EDITOR.

an appointment in either department was and is still the same.

The condition for entering the university as a regular student is here, as everywhere else in Germany, a diploma testifying that the candidate successfully passed the course of a gymnasium.

The course of the academic study comprehends four years, while a triennium is sufficient in nearly all the other German states. The fact which accounts for this difference in time is that in Bavaria the student is expected to devote one year, and generally the first one, to improving his general education. He may gather the best fruits in philosophy, philology, or natural sciences, and then, elevated by the impression that all branches of human knowledge receive their vital force from the same roots, he commences his professional study with brighter hopes and greater satisfaction.

The four years' study at the university are the first and merely theoretical part of the preparation for the civil service. The conclusion of this first part is the so-called theoretical examination of the following subjects:

1. Philosophy of law.
2. Roman civil law.
3. German private law.
4. Civil procedure.
5. Criminal law.
6. Criminal procedure.
7. Public law of the German Empire and of the kingdom of Bavaria.
8. Law of the Catholic and Protestant Churches.
9. Science and law of police.
10. Political economy.
11. Finance.

The commission in charge of the examination consists of a government delegate who has the chair, and six or eight professors of the university. The examination is oral and public. The majority of the audience is composed of students. Each of the eleven subjects receives equally careful attention by the examiners. The candidate whose knowledge has satisfied this commission **enters upon** the three years' course of his practical preparation.

He has to serve twelve months in one of **the** administrative departments, eighteen months at the courts and six months in the office of an attorney-at-law. But wherever he is employed, an account of his work is faithfully kept, which will testify that the candidate is sufficiently prepared to pass the second or practical examination. This time he has to pass a **written** and oral examination, and the former is of greater importance than the latter. It lasts **twelve** days and covers the same subjects as the theoretical examination. The candidates are under continual supervision of one of the commissioners, and the time is limited to eight or nine hours a day. They have **to** grapple with complicated and extensive cases of private and public law and with the problems of the day **in political** economy and finance.

The commission consists of officers of high rank **in** the judicial, administrative and finance departments. Having successfully passed this second trial the candidate is at liberty **to** select his special profession and the department he intends **to enter.** He who **will** become a notary has to serve two **more years in** the office **of a** notary, before he can be employed; and the financial service requires **the** candidate to work six months further **in** a court of claims, and then undergo a third examination on the subject of financial administration.

WÜRTEMBERG.

It is a principle established **by the** Constitution of Würtemberg (1819) that those only can obtain an office under the government who successfully pass the prescribed examinations. In 1817 the faculty of political science of the university of Tübingen was founded to educate young men for the service.

Men generally study four years, though three and a half years is required by law. This university course is of such a high quality and prepares the student so thoroughly that the succeeding practical course is limited to one year and a half.

The rules now in force were issued November 7, 1885. The first examination takes place after the university course has been completed, and is conducted by six university professors and one government commissioner.

They examine in the following subjects:
1. Private law of Würtemberg.
2. Penal law.
3. Mode of procedure in civil and penal law.
4. Public law of the empire of Germany and of the kingdom of Würtemberg.
5. Law of the Protestant and Catholic Churches.
6. Political economy.
7. Administration.
8. Administrative law of Germany and Würtemburg.

The second examination at the end of the practical course is conducted by a board of examiners, composed of officers in the Department of the Interior, who are appointed by the minister. It is a written and oral examination. In the former, the applicants have to treat cases in administration, administrative and penal law and to answer questions on the theory and law of taxation and finance. The oral examination covers the eight subjects enumerated above with addition of taxation, law of taxation in Würtemberg, and finance.

BADEN.

The civil service of Baden is regulated by a law of December 16, 1853, which underwent several changes before August 11, 1883.

The university course extends over three and a half years and the practical course lasts three years. In the two examinations, the one at the end of the university course and the other after the practical preparation, the examining boards are composed of officers of the interior and judicial ministries, with the exclusion of professors. With regard to the university course the applicant has to observe the following rules:

He must attend lectures on nineteen subjects: three lectures in the philosophical faculty, five lectures in political science (philosophy of law, public law, political economy, theory of police and finance), and eleven lectures on subjects of law. The first examination is oral and written. The written examination covers sixteen subjects of law and political science. Fifty-five questions are asked and one hour is allowed for each question. These questions are classified in the following way: Roman private law, eight questions: history of Roman law, three; civil law of France and Baden, six; civil law of Germany, five; public law, four; church law, two; procedure in civil law, five; penal law, five; procedure in penal law, four; philosophy of law, two; political economy, four; science of police, four; finance, three. The oral examination includes civil law of Rome, France and Baden; procedure in civil law, penal law and political economy.

The practical preparation is regulated as follows: twelve months of service in district courts, eight months in the supreme court (*Oberlandesgericht*), twelve months in the administrative department and four months in the office of a lawyer.

The second examination covers the law of Baden, including constitutional and administrative law. In the oral examination the applicant has to give a report of a practical case.

KINGDOM OF SAXONY.

The law of July 20, 1859, enumerates the subjects to which the student has to devote his attention. They are: public law of Saxony, international law, politics, theory of police, administrative law of the kingdom, statistics, political economy, finance, technology, theory of agriculture and forestry. The entire course of preparation is very similar to that of the South German states as outlined above. A written and oral examination is required at the end of the academic study of about the same character as that in Bavaria and Würtemberg. This examination is conducted by professors of the University of Leipzig. Four years of practical service follow, with an examination at the conclusion, which is conducted by a board of examiners composed of administrative officers.

PRUSSIA.

A law of May 6, 1869, regulates the preparation for the civil service of Prussia.

Two examinations have to be passed on the course that leads to the civil service. In the first, which occurs at the end of the academic career, the candidate has to give account of the quantity and quality of knowledge he acquired while listening to the teachings of the professors. In the second trial, which is to be passed four years later, the practical capacity of the candidate is tested. In both cases the examining board is composed of government officers. The first examination is oral and written, and the subjects are: the various descriptions of public and private law, history of law and principles of political science. The candidate who successfully passed this examination has to serve two years in a bureau of the judicial department and two years in a bureau of the administrative department. Then the second examination in written and oral form takes place. It covers the following subjects: public and private law of Prussia, especially constitutional and administrative law, political economy and finance.

GENERAL FEATURES.

In all the German states the preparatory course for the administrative and judicial careers is alike; we see that greatest importance is attributed to legal education and that only a second place is assigned to political science. This relation will not long continue to exist, for the life of the people calls for political science. New forces of life have been created. They require new forms, new laws, new organizations. The art of government becomes more difficult every day and the saying that "a public office is a public trust" daily receives more significance in Germany as in America. It is ridiculous to fight giants with an army of dwarfs. We have to train an army of public servants that shall be equal to those hosts. This can only be done with the help of political science. All the legal knowledge in the world will not enable us to solve the problem of pauperism, nor to regulate organizations of labor, to make provisions for accidents, to decide the questions of protection or free-trade and finance. Consequently the demand that the officer should have thoroughly studied social and economic science becomes more imperative every day.

In all German states a theoretical and practical course is required. This extends the entire preparation to seven or eight years. The office is no sinecure, no easy prey for those persons who have failed by incapacity or idleness in other fields of activity. Great sacrifices are imposed upon public servants, sacrifices never to be remunerated with money. Intellectual capacity and moral character are severely tested before men are admitted to the lowest position. Their recompense is the feeling that they are a part in the great national organism, that they can use all their power for the welfare of the nation, and that they belong to a class of men most highly respected in all the world. It would, indeed, be possible to unite both ways of education more closely. And the ideal will always be an academy of political science, where, as in military and naval academies, the newly-gained theoretical knowledge is immediately applied in practice. Into the practical course, as it is now, a greater division of labor might enter, and the candidates be prepared for a special department. They might become acquainted with certain branches of industrial life, as banking, exports and imports, coinage, etc.

On the whole we may say that Germany is one of the best governed countries in the world, because she has the best developed civil service. It is the latter that determines to a certain degree to-day the political character of a state. We know that the best laws are worthless, that the work of intelligent legislators is frustrated, that the will of the people is not fulfilled, if the officers to whom we entrust the execution of the laws represent notorious incapacity. Even the intentions of a good constitution are checked by the sins of commission and omission in a bad administration.

LIST OF BOOKS UPON THE CIVIL SERVICE OF GERMANY.

Robert Mohl, über die wissenschaftliche Bildung der Beamten in den Ministerien des Innern. Zeitschrift für die gesamte Staatswissenschaft, 1845.

Robert Mohl, über eine Anstalt zur Bildung höhrer Staatsdiener, id.

Ernst Engel, das statistische Seminar des K. preussischen Bureaus in Berlin, 1864.

Erwin Nasse, über das Universitätsstudium der preussischen Verwaltungsbeamten. Bonn, 1868.

Albert Schäffle, zur Frage der Prüfungsansprüche an die Kandidaten des höheren Staatsdienstes, Zeitschrift für die gesamte Staatswissenschaft, 1868.

Georg Meyer, das Studium des öffentlichen Rechts- und der Staatswissenschaften in Deutschland. Jena, 1875.

Lorenz von Stein, die staatswissenschaftliche und die landwirtschaftliche Bildung. Breslau, 1880.

Lorenz von Stein, Gegenwart und Zukunft der Rechts- und der Staatswissenschaft Deutschlands. Stuttgart, 1875.

Ludwig Jolly, die Ausbildung der Verwaltungsbeamten. Zeitschrift für die gesamte Staatswissenschaft, 1875.

Gustav Cohn, über eine akademische Vorbildung zum höhren Eisenbahnverwaltungsdienste. Zürich, 1876.

Gustav Cohn, Ueber das staatswissenschaftliche Studium der preussischen Verwaltungsbeamten. Archiv für Eisenbahnwesen, 1885.

Adolph Wagner, zur Statistik und zur Frage der Einrichtung des national-ökonomischen und statistischen Unterrichts an den deutschen Universitäten, Zeitschrift des K. statischen Bureaus. 1877.

L. Goldschmidt, das dreijährige Studium der Rechts- und Staatswissenschaften. Berlin, 1878.

Otto Gierke, die Juristische Studienordnung. Jahrbuch für Gesetzgebung, Verwaltung und Volkswirtschaft, 1877.

Rudolf Gneist, die Studien- und Prüfungsordnung der deutschen Juristen. Berlin, 1878.

Joh. Friedr. von Schulte, Gedanken über Aufgabe und Reform des Juristischen Studiums.

G. Blondel, de l'enseignement du droit dans les universités allemandes. Paris, 1886.

Dernburg, die Reform der Juristischen Studienordnung. Berlin, 1886.

Dr. Franz v. Liszt, Reform des Juristischen Studiums. Berlin, 1886.

Dr. Leonhard, Noch ein Wort über den Juristischen Universitätsunterricht. Marburg, 1887.

Die Vorbildung zum höheren Verwaltungsdienste in den deutschen Staaten, Oesterreich und Frankreich. Berichte und Gutachten ueröffentlicht vom Verein für Socialpolitik. Leipzig, 1887.

L. Goldschmidt, Rechtsstudium und Prüfungsordnung, ein Beitrag zur preussischen und deutschen Rechtsgeschichte. Stuttgart, 1887.

G. Cohn, über die Vorbildung zum höheren Verwaltungsdienste in den deutschen Staaten. Zeitschrift für die gesammte Staatswissenschaft, 1887.

www.ingramcontent.com/pod-product-compliance
Lightning Source LLC
Chambersburg PA
CBHW020234090426
42735CB00010B/1695